Echoes of Inspiration
Journal Thoughts – Volume One
By Dr. Donald R. Hudson

Copyright ©2016 Donald R. Hudson
Indianapolis, Indiana USA

Unless otherwise indicated, all Scripture quotations are taken from the King James Version of The Holy Bible. Also taken from The Holy Bible, English Standard Version® (ESV®) Copyright © 2001 by Crossway, a publishing ministry of Good News Publishers.

Your purchase of the *Echoes of Inspiration* is for your own personal use. You may not copy it, either for resale or to give away to others. Making copies, either for resale or to give away, is a violation of United States copyright law.

Publication production provided by Vision Communications
www.VisioncomSolutions.com

PUBLISHED BY

DEDICATION

This work is dedicated to my loving wife, *Leatrice*, and my two wonderful and gifted daughters, *Zuri* and *Zenobia*. I learn much from you about the treasures and measures of life. To my granddaughter *Amari*, you add another meaning to inspiration in your small way.

To those of you who dare press beyond the difficulties of time with an aspiration to see what the future holds.

To those of you who continually chisel out masterpieces from your granite experiences.

To those of you who have stopped along the way for some reason or another, but refuse to stand still.

To those of you who have gotten lost in the fog of your faith, but continually search for clarity and meaning.

To those who continually search for an alternative reality.

To you I write.

Contents

Dedication	
Introduction	
In Divine Favor	9
Don't Forget To Say Thanks	12
Making It through the Maze	15
Successful Failures	18
Using Time Wisely	21
Faith	24
Swimming against the Currents	27
It's A Wonder	30
Turns and Curves	33
Caught In Between	36
Determination	39
Facing the Winds	42
Dealing with Life Trials	45
Writing New Stories and Shaping New Experiences	48
It's A New Day	51
Choosing Defeat or Victory	54
Life Questions	57
Facing Life Challenges	60
Don't Forget How Blessed You Are	63
Opportunities	66
Caught In Trivia Traffic	69
Trusting God	72
Making Life Work	75
Dealing with Life Disappointments	78

CONTENTS Continued...

Bouncing Back From Disappointments	81
In God's Awesomeness	84
Becoming a New Creation	87
When Deep Calls To Deep	90
Going Beyond Contentment	93
We Are That Place	96
Dealing with Giants, Battles, Fears and Failures	99
Facing Mountains and Valleys	102
Resilience	106
Getting Reconnected	109
When Life Says No	112
In Pursuit Of Happiness	115
In Pursuit Of Peace	119
Fulfilling Your Destiny	121
Divine Providence	124
Waiting for Something Worthwhile	127
Overcoming Life's Obstacles	130
Pressing On Anyhow	133
Keeping Balance	136
Playing the Cards You Are Dealt	139
Controlling the Effects of Your Pain	143
Taking Hold of the New	146
The Power of Your Mind	148
Living in Expectations	151
It Starts with One Day at a Time	154
Taking Control of the Direction You Go	157
Facing God	160
Life's Notebook	163
Letter from the Author	166
About the Author	168

INTRODUCTION

Everyone needs to be inspired from time to time. Inspiration gives us the hope we need in order to press beyond where we are in life to new levels of experiences. It gives us the momentum to keep pushing forward beyond the obstacles we face.

Inspiration has power. The power of inspiration is timeless and endless. It's timeless and endless in that it is not limited to the timing of this mortal world. Inspiration has eternal potential. When we are inspired we are enabled to see glimpses of another world beyond the world in which we live which offers us hope. In some way or another it is connected to God. God is all inspiring.

When we are inspired whether it come by way of family, friends, or strangers, or from a book, or a song, or by way of something as simple as the morning sun peeping through a window after a nightly storm, or by way of a simple unexpected hug from a child, or by the fragrance of fresh fallen rain on a spring morning, or just from silence – inspiration empowers us, as well as encourage us to attempt to do those things we are sometimes too afraid to tackle.

Inspiration is that stimulus or compelling power we receive in order to climb out of life's valleys and reach for some pinnacle point in life. It is that breath of fresh air that gives us the strength to go the extra mile when we are feeling weary. One could say that inspiration is the wind beneath our wings that gives us the power to fly even when our wings are wounded.

This book is composed of raw journal pieces. It is a collection of thoughts, and encouraging words and phrases written to inspire and stimulate the mind, emotions, spirit and soul towards reaching for the best that life has to offer. In times such as these that are capable of pulling our attention from the positive and the powerful, we are in need of inspiration.

The words offered in this simple book are composed of thoughts that may not run parallel with grammatical correctness and order. It is my intention as the author to keep what is recorded on these pages as close to their original form – when they were fresh, uncut and undisturbed by logic and rationale. This was done intentionally in order to maintain the rhyme of my thoughts and feelings at the time I wrote them.

Writing these journal entries gave me the strength, faith and courage not to give up on what I believe has meaning and purpose. Journaling our thoughts can be the light we need that inspires us to press through and out of those dark places when we feel pressed to the earth. Such pressing encounters have nothing to do with our religious or spiritual aptitude. It is simply a part of our human journey. It's a natural part of our human existence. It's a way of life.

The journal pieces recorded in this first volume are a limited collection of my personal journal entries written over the years that connect to real life issues, joys, pains, fears and expectations that are seldom expressed openly. It's a mixture of spiritual thoughts, and real life feelings that remind us of those precious and special moments and events we have encountered, but sometime forget or choose not to remember as we journey through our often complicated, rushed and hurried schedules, as we attempt to make sense of life.

This first volume is composed of fifty two inspirational pieces for meditation, one for each week of the year. We learn many things by rehearsal and meditation. I hope that you will take the time through the course of a week to digest each inspirational piece individually. Each piece is accompanied by Scriptures from the New International Version of the Bible (NIV) for devotional reading, followed by a simple prayer and questions that can inspire one toward their own personal journaling.

I hope that the words expressed on these pages, will remind you that the Creator is forever present in your daily affairs and desire for you, the best that life has to offer as you face life head-on through faith. I hope that this book inspires you to recapture life that is a gift from God. I hope that these somewhat sporadic thoughts will encourage you to face your real issues and see the great possibilities that lay beyond them.

As you read these words I hope you will be inspired to revisit, recollect, reflect and revaluate the various experiences of your life whether they are large or small, simple or complex, boring or dramatic, negative or positive, in order to discover their truest meaning and purpose. Perhaps you will discover something about yourself and that is, that you are a unique creation of God and that it is alright to be you and that your definition of yourself is more powerful than the definitions others and your experiences place upon you. As you read the words of this collection of thoughts, allow yourself to become a volume of inspiration to others, for as we inspire others, we are inspired.

One of the greatest quests that we can venture towards is that of searching for inspiration as we dig for the meaning and purpose of life. Life without inspiration becomes boring and uneventful.

Being inspired is not automatic, neither is it free.

To be inspired, we must desire it to the point that we search for it with diligence and faith.

Being inspired comes with a cost. We cannot hold on to those things that weigh us down and expect to be inspired to be more, do more and receive more. We must be willing to pay the price of letting go of some things, if we are going to reach the very best that God desires for us – and that is reaching some pinnacle in life even if we have to reach it alone – just us and the Creator.

Welcome to Echoes of Inspiration!

# In Divine Favor

This constitutes the romance of life. At every bend of the road there are new unfolding, and each new day reveals undiscovered grandeurs. Life holds many surprises.

JOSEPH R. SIZOO

There are times when we find ourselves in the midst of Divine favor. We don't always recognize it at the offset – at the beginning. Some kind of way and at some point we come to realize that the events that occurred in our lives that are connected to our past did not occur by happenstance or by accident. They are all a part of the process of God's divine favor.

Each experience, every episode and each occurrence that takes place in our lives, were and is, and will be for the purpose of pushing us towards the ultimate purpose for which we are created. Had it not been for our yesterdays, whether positive or negative we wouldn't think and act the way we do, or be where we are. Whether our past or present is negative or positive, in the hands God it leads to His favor. As we continue to press through the day whether hard or rough, pleasurable or painful, with tears or with smiles, we should remember that the Creator's hand of favor is on us during the whole journey, working things out on our behalf. Therefore, we should without hesitation praise and thank Him that we are able to glean in fields of His divine favor regardless of where we've been in life or where we are in this journey. For we know that by God's favor we have a future.

SCRIPTURE FOR MEDITATION

For the Lord God is a sun and shield; the Lord bestows favor and honor; no good things does he withhold from those whose walk is blameless.

Psalm 84:11

PRAYER

Lord, I pray that you will teach me to recognize your favor. Show me how not to take your favor in vain. Show me how to be still and trust you knowing that every experience that I encounter leads me to your favor. Amen.

Personal Journal Thoughts:

What does God's favor mean to you? How do you see God's favor in your life and what will you do with it?

_____
_____
_____
_____
_____
_____
_____
_____
_____
_____
_____
_____
_____
_____
_____
_____
_____
_____
_____
_____
_____

Don't Forget To Say Thanks

O Lord, that lends me life, Lend me a heart replete with thankfulness.
                                   WILLIAM SHAKESPEARE

Sometimes it's easy to get lost in the blessings that are bestowed upon us by God. From my perspective such loss is not due to some ungrateful spirit. Instead, there are times when we become so overwhelmed or even excited about all that God has done for us, that we lose focus on He who has granted us His blessings. If we are not careful we will thank others and forget to say thank you to God who has been our Ultimate Provider. When this occurs we should remind ourselves to slow down and get out of the rat race and reflect on God's goodness and count our blessings, if it is at all possible to count them, and simply say thanks. After all, saying thanks makes room for more.

We should never become so caught up in the blessings we've received to the point that we fail to pause and give thanks to Him who blesses us. Being mindful of God who blesses us shows a sense of gratitude that opens doors that leads to more.

SCRIPTURE FOR MEDITATION

Enter his gates with thanksgiving and his courts with praise; give thanks to him and praise his name. For the Lord is good and his love endures forever; his faithfulness continues through all generations.

Psalm 100:4-5

PRAYER

Dear heavenly Father, I come to you with thanksgiving. Thank you for all you have done for me. Your grace and mercy follows me all day long. Create in me a thankful heart. I will never forget how kind you are to me. Thank you for being my God and supplying my needs according to your riches in glory through Christ. Amen.

Personal Journal Thoughts:

What are the things you thank God for? What can you do to express your deepest thanks to God?

 ## Making It through the Maze

Even at the worst there is a way out, a hidden secret that can turn failure into success and despair into happiness. No situation is so dark that there is not a ray of light.

NORMAN VINCENT PEALE

Finding our way through this maze we call life is not an easy task. Often times the maze of life is composed of turns, curves, twist and dead ends we do not anticipate or even plan for. It is usually during these unanticipated times and unplanned for moments that we get lost in the way we are traveling – failing at the curves and going down dead ends and even hitting walls. But, we should refuse and deny the temptation to stop pressing to find the exit. When we continue to fight the temptation of giving in and giving out, we will discover that God will lead us to our appointed destiny if we would only trust in Him and keep the faith that He will never leave us alone, even when we get lost in the maze. We should remember that God will not allow us to enter a place in life that He has not already provided us a way out. Our task is to keep moving forward as best we can without giving in or giving out, because we have to keep going, even if we have to go at it alone.

SCRIPTURE FOR MEDITATION

Trust in the Lord with all your heart and lean not on your own understanding; in all your ways acknowledge him, and he will make your path straight.
Proverbs 3:5-6

PRAYER

Lord, I come to you saying, thanks for being my God. I confess that there are times when I get lost in this world. Guide me according to your presence. Give me direction in the way that I should go. If I should get off track, show me the right path, and when I run into a dead end, turn me around by your grace. Amen

Personal Journal Thoughts:

What do you consider are the mazes of your life and how do you intend to get through them?

Successful Failures

The rung of a ladder was never meant to rest upon, but only to hold a man's foot long enough to enable him to put the other somewhat higher.

THOMAS HENRY HUXLEY

All the failures in life are not simply those who have never tried their hands at something, neither are they those who tried their hand at something and decided to give up in the process. But some who fail are successful – successful failures.

Successful failures are those of us who have accomplished something great – reached a particular goal – gotten the position we always wanted – gotten the promotion or the job we've worked hard for or received the manifestation of our dreams, only to stop where we are to enjoy our accomplishments too long, and never pushing forward to any other venture. Yes! We can be successful, but we can also fail at receiving or experiencing the rest of what God has for us. So, I guess the proper thing to do is to keep pressing life until it runs out, least we become successful failures. After all, life has more to offer beyond where we are presently, even if we are successful in what we are doing. We should never stop moving forward until we have reached the summit of the life God has given us.

SCRIPTURE FOR MEDITATIONS

Commit to the Lord whatever you do, and your plans will succeed. The Lord works out everything for his own ends – even the wicked for a day of disaster.

Proverbs 16:3-4

PRAYER

Lord, thank you for all you have allowed me to accomplish. I realize that my successes have been due to your power. Give me the courage to press to the next level and not settle for where I am. Lord, I know that you have more for me. Give me the courage to reach for the highest star. Amen.

Personal Journal Thoughts:

How do you define your success? Is there more that you can do? What will you do in order to take your life to its highest?

 # Using Time Wisely

Spend your time in nothing which you know must be repented of; in nothing on which you might not pray for the blessing of God; in nothing which you could not review with a quiet conscience on your dying bed; in nothing which you might not safely and properly be found doing if death should surprise you in the act.

RICHARD BAXTER

It amazes me how we can get side tracked even in the things that seems to be the right thing to do. I guess we can fill our plates with so much stuff and forget or overlook the most important things. I'm realizing that great tasks without great focus can equal a great loss of time and energy. Perhaps one of the overlooked sins is our misuse of time. When we recapture time as it relates to using it wisely, we recapture life. Sometimes one has to slow down and get a real picture of where they are, in order to move forward and re-adjust their life and time least life becomes trapped in the mar of sameness and mediocrity even when things are well. We should use our time to make life its best.

SCRIPTURE FOR MEDITATION

Sow your seed in the morning, and at evening let not your hands be idle, for you do not know which will succeed, whether this or that, or whether both will do equally well.
                                                                Ecclesiastes 11:6

PRAYER

Dear heavenly Father, thank you for life and time. I confess that there have been times when I did not use my time wisely. Please forgive me. Show me how not to take the time you have given me for granted. I realize that time is a gift from you. Give me the wisdom to take the advantage of the blessings of time. Amen.

Personal Journal Thoughts:

How well do you use your time? What can you do in order to make the best use of your time?

 *Faith*

Faith is like a boomerang; begin using what you have and it comes back to you in greater measure.

CHARLES L. ALLEN

Faith is a funny thing. It never works until it takes on the faculties of who we are and what we genuinely believe. I believe that faith shows itself in various forms. First, it shows up in our proclamation of what we believe is true or will become a reality. Our faith is displayed in the words we speak. It is heard in the words we use to describe our day and our experiences, as well as our expectations. It shows in what we say before an event takes place and shape.

Secondly, our faith is displayed in what we look for in life and what we look forward to as it relate to our expectations as our hope expands towards the future. Genuine faith can never be detached from the future, if it's real faith.

Thirdly, our faith is displayed based upon what we attempt. We are told in Scripture that faith without works is dead. Our faith never grows until we sometimes take on a task that is sometimes bigger than we are.

Faith starts with what we say, and then with what we expect and then with what we attempt to do for ourselves and for others. Out of these three dynamics of faith, our faith grows and manifests those things we hope for, as we continue to trust in Christ who is the author and the finisher of our faith.

Faith is the hallmark of what we really believe about God, as well as what we believe about ourselves as we trust in our God given abilities.

SCRIPTURE FOR MEDITATION

We live by faith, not by sight.

2 Corinthians 5:7

PRAYER

Lord, increase my faith. I admit that the troubles of life sometimes cause my faith to become weak. Show me what it means to trust you with all of my whole heart. I believe that you are faithful to your promises. Show me how to enlarge my faith that brings you glory and that causes life to become complete. Amen.

Personal Journal Thoughts:

How deep is your faith? In what area does your faith need to increase? What can you do to increase your faith? What areas do you need apply more faith?

Swimming against the Currents

Courage is the first of human qualities because it is the quality which guarantees all the others.
WINSTON CHURCHCHILL

Sometimes we find ourselves caught in the currents where two rivers meet – human fright and our expectations of the future. I have come to realize that human fright is a natural part of our human makeup. Such fright is not always due to our mistrust in God, it's just a glitch in our human armor and the fact that we are simply human. But, those of us who truly trust God as much as possible take the chance to swim against the currents regardless of how frightful it can be at times. Currents have the tendency to scare the best swimmers.

We dare swim against life currents in expectation, finally reaching our faith in God who gives us grace to beat our fears of the unexpected.

We sometimes find ourselves fighting the currents that seek to push us back into fear and discouragement. But, if we continue to trust in God no matter how deep the waters are or how rough the currents get, God will not allow us to be taken under.

The currents of life can be dealt with successfully no matter how rough they are. It takes faith and determination to deal with the currents we face. With God we will get through the currents we encounter in life. God has for those who trust Him, more rivers to cross, seas and oceans to explore with success. He has given us the ability and the courage to swim through the currents regardless of how rough the waters seem.

SCRIPTURE FOR MEDITATION

The Lord is my strength and my shield; my heart trusts in him, and I am helped. My heart leaps for joy and I will give thanks to him in song.

Psalm 28:7

PRAYER

Lord, I get tired sometimes as I swim amidst the currents. Sometimes I don't know if I can make it. Give me the courage and the strength to keep moving forward and not go under. Help me when I am weak and discouraged. Never allow me to go under without coming back up. Amen.

Personal Journal Thoughts:

What do you consider as the currents on your life? What can you do in order the make it through the currents you face?

 *It's A Wonder*

Perhaps history is a thing that would stop happening if God held His breath.

HERBERT BUTTERFIELD

We should praise God for waking us up each morning in spite of our falling and failures the previous day. When we look at ourselves it's a wonder that God has not given up on us.

It's a wonder that God continues to provide us with His favor in spite of our ungratefulness for that which He has already provided.

It's a wonder that we have not lost our minds amidst the craziness of this world.

It's a wonder that we have not gone over the edge or slipped into some abyss.

It's a wonder that God hasn't abandoned us even when we abandon him. He promised never to leave us and he hasn't.

Therefore, since God who is perfect in all His ways, believes in us, we should learn to humor Him by believing in ourselves and attempt to use all that He has provided, and have bestowed upon us for His glory with much thankfulness.

SCRIPTURE FOR MEDITATION

O Lord God Almighty, who is like you? You are Almighty, O Lord, and your faithfulness surrounds you.

Psalm 89:8

PRAYER

Lord, how great is your power! Each morning I wake up I see the wonderful works of your hands. You are all powerful. You have no limitations. I offer to you glory for the wonders you have allowed my eyes to behold. When I look at myself I see a creation made by your hands. Glory to your name! Amen.

Personal Journal Thoughts:

How do you see and define the wonders of God in your life? How do you respond to God's wonders?

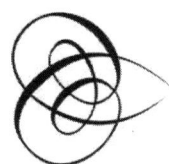 *Turns and Curves*

We shall steer safely through every storm, so long as our heart is right, our intention fervent, our courage steadfast, and our trust fixed on God.

ST. FRANCIS DE SALES

Sometimes life takes a turn and it's in the curves where we are usually taken for a spin. Sometimes when we are caught in a spin the only resolution we have is to hold on as tightly as possible until it all slows down or until in some way or another we regain control of those situations that threw us for a loop. Either way, in life we must spin. But, we have been given the power to regain control in spite of the unexpected turns and curves we experience. Living a life out of control and with no direction is not an option for the faithful. When we think about it, the turns in life is not all bad, for without them life is not fun or eventful, neither rewarding.
We should remember that turns and curves test the stability of our faith in God who is in control of all things.

SCRIPTURE FOR MEDITATION

Every valley shall be filled in, every mountain and hill made low. The crooked roads shall become straight, the rough ways smooth. And all mankind will see God's salvation.
Luke 3:5-6

PRAYER

Dear Heavenly Father, guide my way. There are times when I lose it in the turns and the curves in life. Make my way plain by your grace and mercy. Keep me on the right path in order that I may not lose my way. Amen.

Personal Journal Thoughts:

What can you do in order to deal successfully with the turns and curves you face?

Caught In Between

Not for one single day can I discern my way, but this I surely know – Who gives the day will show the way, so I surely go.
JOHN OXENHAM

Some days we awake and wonder how and when did we arrive at some unfamiliar place? Life is a funny and sometimes unidentifiable event. No name for it!

We awake and sometimes find ourselves standing between two polarities; such as, wanting to know the truth, and wanting to run from reality; shame and confession, victories and defeat, mistrust and faithfulness, wanting to be real and the temptation to fake it. This is when we desire to get out of the flow of the real deal of things. I believe this is due to the fact that we sometimes contend that perhaps God is finished making us into someone better than who we are. Such thoughts lead to some type of death. We can't live life as if God is finished with us, least we pause too long between here and there and miss the rest that God has for us. If we do, we die in some way or another.

We must fight the temptation to quit, because life gets hard at times. This is not an easy task to accomplish. It's not easy to be still when we are caught in between the present and the unknown. But, it can be done. We should remember that when we find ourselves caught in between some rock and a hard place, we must be determined to hold on until our change come, for this is when we discover that God is in the process of blessing us to move to new levels. We must simply trust God long enough until we find our way out.

SCRIPTURE FOR MEDITATION

Though he slay me, yet will I hope in him; I will surely defend my ways to his face. Indeed, this will turn out for my deliverance ...

Job 13:15-16

PRAYER

Dear heavenly Father, I praise you for life. I praise you for every experience I encounter. Sometimes I find myself caught in the middle of life with no human answers to the things I face. But, you are my Father and I know that you will work all things out for my good and for your glory. So, Farther I trust you as I keep moving forward even though I may not understand all the things that may occur. Amen.

Personal Journal Thoughts:

How's your faith in God when you find yourself caught in between faith and fear? How do you view the presence of God when you are caught between the present and the future?

Determination

With all the infinite possibilities of spiritual life before you, do not settle down on a little patch of dusty ground at the mountain's foot in restful content. Be not content until you reach the mountain's summit.

J. R. MILLER

One of the strongest factors in life is that of determination. Determination makes a difference no matter how you look at it. I believe that without determination we fail to reach the pinnacles of life. Man fails to reach his fullest potential if he has no determination to press against the odds that stands to barricade him from his destiny. His abilities are only half used when determination is absent. There are enemies of the determined soul:
- Depression
- A lack of a focused mind
- A purposeless life
- Fear
- Procrastination
- No plan

If one is to stay determined and stay his course the following should exist in his life.

- *Happiness and Peace*, regardless of the storm. Happiness and Peace is like oxygen is to our lungs.
- *Focus*, this allows us to keep our aim in the right direction.
- Purposeful life, life without purpose goes nowhere. Therefore, we should seek to discover our purpose in life. We all exist for a greater reason.
- *Valor*, if we are to reach the pinnacles of life, we must learn to stand against the odds and fight the spirit of fear.
- *Persistency*, we can't reach new levels when we continue stop before we reach the summit of our lives. We cannot always wait until tomorrow, for tomorrow is not promised. We must be determined to take advantage of today. Opportunities come, but they do not linger.
- *Planning*, where there is no plan life stops in its tracks and we miss the rest of what God has for us. Planning is a step towards success.

SCRIPTURE FOR MEDITATION

So do not throw away your confidence; it will be richly rewarded. You need to persevere so that when you have done the will of God, you will receive what he has promised.
Hebrews 10:35-36

PRAYER

Lord, it is hard to press on some times. Sometimes my faith fades in the midst of trouble and I feel like giving up. But, you have kept me strong. Please give me the power through the Holy Spirit and in your promises in order that I may continue to press towards the goals you have placed before me. I refuse to give up, for I trust in your Word. Amen.

Personal Journal Thoughts:

How determined are you? What are you determined for? What will you do in order to reach those things for which you are created?

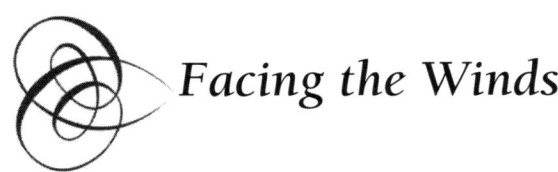# Facing the Winds

Faith is an assurance inwardly prompted, springing from the irrepressible impulse to do, to fight, to triumph.

GEORGE SANTAYANA

At times, the events in life come like a wind from all four directions. Some winds are expected, while others come as a surprise. Some winds are of our own making, while others come naturally or even composed by others. Whether they come expectantly or by surprise, whether they are something we composed in our own life, or the making of nature, or composed by others, the winds of life are inevitable. They must be!

Sometimes we have no plan or clue as to how we will handle our windy encounters. For those of us who trust in God, winds are ways that propels us to the best possibilities that our Father has in store for us. When we are in the hands of God, He use the winds we face to push us to the next level.

The best thing to do when we find ourselves caught in the winds, is to tie our ropes tighter and hoist our sails as high as possible and head for the open seas in order to see what else God has in store for us. Winds are not all bad, when we use them for our advantage.

SCRIPTURE FOR MEDITATION

Whoever watches the wind will not plant; who looks at the clouds will not reap. As you do not know the path of the wind, or how the body is formed in a mother's womb, so you cannot understand the work of God, the Maker of all things.

Ecclesiastes 11:4-5

PRAYER

Dear heavenly Father, I'm sometimes blown upon by the winds of life that test my faith. Sometimes I become afraid and my faith grows weak. But, I trust you to guide me through the winds. I admit that it gets hard at times, but I have not given up. Please help me to keep going no matter how windy it gets. Amen.

Personal Journal Thoughts:

How do you view the winds in your life? What are they? What can you do in order to deal with the winds you face?

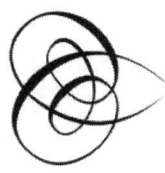 *Dealing with Life Trials*

Your living is determined not so much by what life brings to you as by the attitude you bring to life; not so much by what happens to you as by the way your mind looks at what happens. Circumstances and situations do color life, but you have been given the mind to choose what the colors shall be.
JOHN HOMER MILLER

Somewhere and at some point in life we all face trials whether minor, or major or by our own making, or by the making of others, or simply a result of the rhythm of life. . However, by whatever means they come, we must face them. It is up to us as to how we will deal with the trials that come our way.

- We can allow our trials to alter our attitudes, or we can make our trials into opportunities to develop our strength.
- We can allow our trials to detour us from our destinies, or we can use them as steps toward our destinies.
- We can allow our trials to destroy our faith, or we can use them to develop our faith.

How we respond to our trials is totally left up to us. It's all a matter of choice and faith over our immediate circumstances.

SCRIPTURE FOR MEDITATION

Consider it pure joy ... whenever you face trials ... you know that the testing of your faith develops perseverance. Perseverance must finish its work so that you may be mature and complete, not lacking anything.

James 1:2-4

PRAYER

Dear heavenly Father, thank you for every experience in my life. I even thank you for my trials, for I know that all things have purpose. Father, there are times when I question as to why I go through what I go through. But, your grace and mercy has kept me from giving up. I pray that you will keep me from falling in the way and giving up because things get hard. Keep me in your divine protection. Amen.

Personal Journal Thoughts:

How do you view the trials you face? What purpose do you believe your trials have in your life? What will you do with them?

 *Writing New Stories and Shaping New Experiences*

Everyone shares the responsibility in the future. But this responsibility can materialize into a constructive effort only if people realize the full meaning of their lives, the significance of their endeavors and their struggles, and if they keep their faith in the high destiny of Man.

LECOMTE DU NOUY

It is not where a man comes from that determines the rest of his life. I believe that our lives are determined basically by how we decide to handle the present, and by what we honestly expect in the future in spite of our past.

We cannot change our history. Yesterday has been etched in the stone of time and cannot be erased by any means or by any effort. Whether our past is negative or positive it remains what it is and we must accept it.

However, our present is like a fresh sheet of paper that can be written on, or like fresh clay which can be shaped. If we use our present whether negative or positive to write new stories and to shape new experiences, we can compose and reshape our future into something greater. So, we must be careful of how we use our present. We must choose how we use our "now". It can be wasteful or it can be wonderful. Rewriting our stories and reshaping our lives is a matter of choice. God has given us the creative power to change things, and redirect the way we should go. It is ours to become the author of our own stories and the one who sculpts our future.

SCRIPTURE FOR MEDITATION

Therefore, if anyone is in Christ, he is a new creation; the old has gone, the new has come!

2 Corinthians 5:17

PRAYER

Lord, I come saying thank you for the life you have given me. Thank you for the power to make choices. Through your divine power I have been given the power to choose how my life turns out. Show me how to take control over my circumstances and write a new story according to your power and promises. Show me how to sculpt my tomorrow. Amen.

Personal Journal Thoughts:

Are you satisfied with your life? How can you change your story? How can you sculpture and life that is powerful? What are you willing to do to change your story?

 ## It's A New Day

Every day is a fresh beginning; Listen, my soul, to the glad refrain, And, spite of old sorrow and older sinning, And puzzles forecasted and possible pain, Take heart with the day, and begin again.
                               SUSAN COOLIDGE

Each morning is a blessing we never experienced, waiting to be taken a hold of.

Each day is a new beginning waiting to unfold with new experiences, chances and challenges.

Each of us is given the opportunity to chart out our own destiny – which way we are going to go, as well as to what we will achieve. Charting our destinies is a God given choice.

God gives us everything we need to reach our future. What God gives us may not be what He allows others to have and vice versa. Every man must learn not to think that the grass in someone else's yard is greener than his own, for while he is giving his attention to someone else's grass, his grass grows out of control while choking every opportunity and possibility that is available to him.

We should make it our daily business to thank God for each experience that the day offers us as we chart out our destiny, knowing that we have been given this choice by our Creator who made the heavens and the earth.

We must make it our daily task to take advantage of every new day we are given and not waste it. We should keep close to our chest that once the day has passed it is no more. All we have at our disposal is the present we are allowed to see.

SCRIPTURE FOR MEDITATION

This is the day the Lord has made; let us rejoice and be glad in it.

Psalm 118:24

PRAYER

Lord, thank you for this day. This is the day that the Lord has made! I will rejoice in it! Lord thank you for your kindness towards me. Show me how to move beyond my past and take hold of the present and use it for your glory. Lord! Show me how to live in the now and not in yesterday. Amen.

Personal Journal Thoughts:

How do you view each day you are given? What will you do today that will move you closer to your God given destiny?

Choosing Defeat or Victory

The hero is no braver than an ordinary man, but he is brave five minutes longer.

RALPH WALDO EMERSON

We all are confronted at times with the threat of defeat, particularly for those of us who dare trust in the Divine, and dream that our present can be transformed into something greater.

The option of being defeated is always present. We should understand that defeat is an option and not an absolute. I believe that it is up to us to choose victory over defeat regardless of our situations and the various circumstances we face. This is something I believe God will not choose for us, neither can another. God gives us the choice to choose between victory and defeat. This is a solo task.

We should learn to entertain victory over defeat. What we entertain grows by the attention we give to it. If we entertain defeat, then we lose. If we entertain victory, at some point we will win the battle if we don't quit, even if it takes much time and endless effort. But, defeat should never be an option for the faithful. Defeat is word that should be erased from the pages of the faithful.

SCRIPTURE FOR MEDITATION

...In all these things we are more than conquerors through him who loved us.

Romans 8:37

PRAYER

Lord, I pray that you will give me the power and the wisdom of how not to give up in the battles I face. Show me how to be victorious according to your Word and power that lives in me. Give me the courage to stand firm in my faith. Amen.

Personal Journal Thoughts:

What are the areas in which you feel defeated? What steps will you take to claim victory over those things that defeat you?

 Life Questions

The way of God has properly been described as "letting oneself fall," and has been compared with the first flight of a baby eagle, pushed out of the nest by its parents, and then discovering to its amazement that the invisible ocean of light in which it is dropping is capable of bearing it up. The presence of God which surrounds everyone is like this invisible ocean which bears us up more surely than do all visible means of security.
                                                                    KARL HEIM

We have a tendency to lose our joy in places, people and things that once made us happy, and gave us energy to do something bigger than us. Over a period of time we sometimes lose the happiness in those places, people and things that once put a smile on our face. It is times like these that press us to ask the question as to why we feel the way we feel?

This is the way life is at times and we should not think it strange that such inquiries patterns our way. I don't contend that such questions bespeak of an absent of love for others or for the places we are in. But, perhaps it bespeaks of a deeper love for self, which each of us must discover before we can rise to the next level of our lives and to be a blessing to others. We must move to new levels regardless of where we are at the moment, if we are to discover the new. We cannot wait until things change before we attempt our ascension.

The questions – should I move on or should I stay? These are common inquires that we all face at some point or another. I believe that such questions are signs that we are evolving into someone other than who we used to be or who we are presently. If we ignore such questions or fail to answer them, we may find ourselves existing in places and with people who are no longer a benefit to us or us to them – and find ourselves in places where we're receiving nothing any longer and have nothing to offer.

When we find ourselves faced with such inquiries and with no ready response, we should look to the Creator who will give us the most assured answer – He is God Almighty, for He knows the way that we should take.

SCRIPTURE FOR MEDITATION

Your word is a lamp to my feet and a light for my path. I have taken an oath and confirmed it, that I will follow your righteous laws.

Psalm 119:105-106

PRAYER

Dear heavenly Father, I come to you admitting that there are times when I have many questions about life. I am sometimes confused. Show me how to trust in your Word and your guidance. I know that you have all the answers I need. Help me to be still within myself until your answer comes as I ascend to the next level of my life. Amen.

Personal Journal Thoughts:

What questions to you have about your life? What will you do to find the answers you need as you move to the next level of your life?

 *Facing Life Challenges*

The sun, with all those planets moving round it, can ripen the smallest bunch of grapes as if it had nothing else to do. Why then should I doubt His power?
GALILEO

We all face challenges; some of them are earth shaking while others are mild. Whether earth shaking or mild, we must face them head on and make the right decisions concerning them. These decisions are not always easy, but we should praise God for allowing us to be at a place in life where we can make decisions for ourselves.

Where there is a challenge, we are given by God's grace the potential to handle them. God grants us the power to meet each challenge with victory. We should remember that God never allows us to face anything that we are not strong enough to handle and to overcome, if we are determined to be victorious. We must resolve within ourselves that God never allows us to face a challenge unless He has given us what is needed to subdue them and change them into something for our benefit. Each of us have been given the abilities, talents and gifts to deal with any challenge that comes our way regardless of how it comes or what form it comes in. What we must learn is the art of challenging our challenges.

Instead of fainting because we are challenged, and shrinking in our faith, we should stop and thank God for the challenges we face, for where there are challenges there are chances for success and victory. In addition challenges teach us something about ourselves that is sometimes overlooked in the time of pleasantry.

SCRIPTURE FOR MEDITATION

Do you not know? Have you not heard? The Lord is the everlasting God ... He will not grow tired or weary ... He give strength to the weary and increases the power of the weak. Even youths grow tired and weary ... but those who hope in the Lord ... renew their strength. They will soar on wings like eagles ... run and not grow weary ... walk and not faint.

Isaiah 40:28-31

PRAYER

Lord, I give you all the glory even amongst the challenges I face. Let not my challenges over take me. Show me how to face each challenge without fear but with confidence. You have not given me the spirit of fear, but of power. I stand firm on your promises that sustains me when life gets hard to bear. Amen.

Personal Journal Thoughts:

How do you view your challenges? How will you use your challenges to take you closer to the destiny for which you are created? How do you view the presence of God amidst your challenges?

 Don't Forget How Blessed You Are

Among the many acts of gratitude we owe to God, it may be accounted one to study and contemplate the perfections and beauties of His work of creation. Every new discovery must necessarily raise in us a fresh sense of the greatness, wisdom, and power of God.

JONATHAN EDWARDS

Life offers to us many blessings. If we would stop long enough to count and take inventory of our blessing – if that is at all possible, we will discover how blessed we are. Some of the blessings we receive are sometimes overlooked such as:

Family – Our children or grandchildren sleeping on our bedroom floor, falling asleep after looking at a movie on the television.

Friends – Good friends we can really trust with whom we can laugh and joke with and even cry with, without shame.

Strangers – Kind people we meet along the way, perhaps never to see them on this earth again, who reminds us that our lives are not all bad after all.

Sitting and Listening – Taking the time to sit and listen, while hearing geese flying in the morning, listening to birds singing just before the sun peeps over the Eastern horizon, looking at leaves running across the lawn like race horses in a March wind.

Relationship with God – Just knowing and feeling God's presence. Feeling His love through Jesus who keeps us daily and the Holy Spirit who continues to live in us and who guides us in difficult times.

Life – Just to wake up and know that we are alive.

SCRIPTURE FOR MEDITATION

And my God will meet all your needs according to his glorious riches in Christ Jesus.

Philippians 4:19

PRAYER

Dear heavenly Father, I come to you saying thank you for all you have done for me. Glory to your great name! You have been kind to me and have supplied my needs and have given me the desires of my heart according to your kindness. I will not forget that every good gift comes from you. Thank you for every opportunity and person you have allowed to come into my life to bless me. Amen.

Personal Journal Thoughts:

What do you consider as the blessings in your life and what will you do with them? What can you do to show your thankfulness to God and to others for the blessing you have received?

_____
_____
_____
_____
_____
_____
_____
_____
_____
_____
_____
_____
_____
_____
_____
_____
_____
_____
_____
_____
_____
_____
_____
_____

 *Opportunities*

Today is, for all that we know, the opportunity and occasion of our lives. On what we do or say today may depend the success and completeness of our entire life-struggle. It is for us, therefore, to use every moment of today as if our very eternity were dependent on its words and deeds.
　　　　　　　　　　　　　　　　HENRY CLAY TRUMBULL

God offers us daily opportunities to make life better. He offers us the chance for our lives to be eventful and worth living, as well as the potential to take life to the top. However, if we are not careful and watchful, we can miss our daily opportunities. We should keep in mind that such opportunities for a better and eventful life are not without difficulties. If we renege at taking the chance of the eventful and excitement that is present in life due to our reluctance to face difficult moments, we run the risk of missing the great opportunities that God provides. We sometimes renege at taking advantage of the opportunities made available to us due to the fact that we become overly comfortable with familiarity and sameness and we become reluctant to move out of our comfort zones.

We should learn to put forth the faithful energies we possess and not settle for the less of life, when we can do deeper and greater things.

If we have the potential for mountains the valley will not be pleasing to our souls. Neither will it challenge our mind and energize our potential.

In order to live a life that is pleasing to us and glorifying to God, we must seek to use all that God has given us at any cost. We should make it our daily business and a lifelong venture to take advantage of every good opportunity that comes our way whether they are small or large. If we fail to take advantage of every good opportunity available to us at any cost, it will be costly to us.

SCRIPTURE FOR MEDITATION

Every good and perfect gift is from above, coming down from the Father of the heavenly lights, who does not change like sifting shadows.

James 1:17

PRAYER

Lord, I thank you for this day. I realize that each day is a new day filled with great opportunities. I realize that every good chance that comes my way is from you. You have created me with purpose. Show me how to take advantage of every good opportunity that comes my way and not to take them for granted. Amen

Personal Journal Thoughts:

What opportunities do you have that you are not taking advantage of? If you took advantage of your opportunities, what difference would it make? What are you willing to do in order take advantage of every great opportunity made available to you?

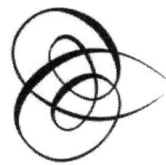 ## Caught In Trivia Traffic

Much may be done in those little shreds and patches of time which every day produces and which most men throw away.

CHARLES CALEB COLTON

There are some mornings when we awake with our heads hanging low and our tails tucked between our legs like a beaten pups. Life just has a way of doing that to us. Much of this has nothing to do with trouble, but with the trivial traffic of life that causes us to waste time when we should be progressing. The best thing to do when caught up in trivial traffic is to exit and go another way as soon as possible.

I believe that time is like the talents given to the three men in the gospel according to Matthew – chapter 25. When we are given the gift of time we should invest it wisely and not waste it. We sometimes feel defeated when we don't use our time wisely, and when we fail to progress in areas where we know we have the potential to move forward. Whenever time is wasted we bury it in unproductive activities and sometimes in meaningless chatter – talk that means nothing. I can't help but believe that this is a sin of some sort. I guess the answer to this is, when we are caught in trivial traffic, and time wasting bumper to bumper commotion – we should take the nearest exit that leads to the path that takes us to progression and productivity.

SCRIPTURE FOR MEDITATION

Forget the former things; do not dwell on the past. See, I am doing a new thing! Now it springs up; do you not perceive it? I am making a way in the desert and streams in the wasteland.

Isaiah 43:18-19

PRAYER

Dear heavenly Father, there are times when I get caught in the traffic of the world and get off track. Sometimes I'm lost and forget my purpose. I confess that sometimes I don't use my time wisely. Forgive me. I ask that you would point me in the right direction in order that I may do your will. When I get caught in the trivial things of life help me to exit and get back on the right path. Amen

Personal Journal Thoughts:

How do you use your time? What are the things in your life that causes you to get caught in the trivia and meaningless things of life? What can you do to escape the trivia?

 *Trusting God*

This is a sane, wholesome, practical, working faith: first, that it is a man's business to do the will of God; secondly, that God takes on himself the special care of that man; and third, that therefore that man ought never to be afraid of anything.

GEORGE MACDONALD

Trusting God is not an easy thing to do. We sometimes face moments when we are totally confused to where exactly God is taking us. Sometimes we are clueless concerning the moments, the moves and even the mountains we face while in the hands of God. All we know is that there is something in us that keep pressing us forward – sometimes in the dark corners of our rationale and logic as it pertains to God's divine movement. It keeps us in those moves God is performing in us and for us. It keeps us ascending our mountains. It's called trust!

I guess the question for each of us is; will we trust God enough to press through the moments, go with the moves and dare to climb the mountains. This I have found to be a task within itself, to just keep trusting God beyond sight and undefined feelings and experiences.
This is not an easy task to perform. I guess this is why it's called trust.

SCRIPTURE FOR MEDITATION

When I am afraid, I will trust in you. In God, whose word I praise, in God I trust; I will not be afraid. What can mortal man do to me?

Psalm 56:3-4

PRAYER

Lord, I admit that trusting you is not always easy. But, in you I put my trust in spite of me not understanding everything that happens in my life and in the lives of those I love. Help me when my trust seems to fade. Give me the strength to stand firm on your promises, because I know that your Word will not fail me. Amen.

Personal Journal Thoughts:

How deep is your trust in God? What do you trust God for? What will you do to display your deepest trust for the things you trust God for?

 *Making Life Work*

God asks no man whether he will accept life. That is not the choice. You must take it. The only choice is how.

HENRY WARD BEECHER

We should make it our business to enjoy life – to make life work. Life offers us many doors in which to enter and many of them are at our finger-tips. Entering the doors available to us does not happen automatically. It is something that we must make up our minds to do if life is going to work out.

The greatest challenge we face is ourselves. We must learn to get past ourselves. We must learn to get beyond **Self- Doubt** - believing that we are not capable of doing great things. We must learn to release **Self-Discrimination** – believing that due to whom God has made us, or even due to what we have allowed ourselves to become, we don't deserve to live better or be better. We must get rid of **Self-Judgment** – always casting a sentence of some form of incarceration upon ourselves because of the guilt of our past, whether it was years ago or just a moment ago. However we look at it, it's the past. We must not become **Self-Destructive** – spending more time creating events and scenarios that causes us to fail as well as putting ourselves in position to be hurt and harmed because it has been the pattern of our life. Lastly, we must not be **Self-Disabling** – practicing habits that causes us to stay within the norm and the prose of life – complacency, apathy, laziness, pity and procrastination.

Instead of us doing these things to ourselves, we should seek to embrace the good things that God has given us – potential, power, abilities, self love, peace, joy, dreams, vision and the energy to live and make life worth living.

SCRIPTURE FOR MEDITATION

Lazy hands make a man poor, but diligent hands bring wealth. He who gathers crops in summer is a wise son, but he who sleeps during harvest is a disgraceful son.
Proverbs 10:4-5

PRAYER

Dear heavenly Father, I come to you saying thank you for life. I realize that life is a gift and should not be taken lightly. Give me your divine directions in how to make life work for your glory. Show me how to use every ability and gift that you have given me. Amen.

Personal Journal Thoughts:

How do you view your life? What can you do to make your life work for the better?

Dealing with Life Disappointments

God's delays are not denials, He has heard your prayer, He knows all about your trials, He knows your very care. God's delays are not denials, help is on the way, He is watching o'er life's dials, bringing forth the day. God's delays are not denials, you will find Him true; working through the darkest trials, what is best for you.

GRACE E. TROY

Sometimes it seems as if there is one disappointment after another. We sometime wonder if it will ever stop. Humanly speaking, we are sometimes disappointed in God, because we cannot readily understand His moves in our lives. We are sometimes disappointed in ourselves and others, as well as disappointed in some of the experiences we have encountered.

If we are not careful our disappointments will determine our attitudes, altitude, personality and powers in life. Our disappointments sometimes can affect our present world and border us from our future possibilities and potential to make life better.

Disappointments are a natural part of life, but for those of us who trust in God, we should view our disappointments as a device of the demonic that seeks to damage our chances for dreams, empowering visions, and chances to live prosperous lives, building healthy families and cultivate meaningful and positive relationships full of nurturing.

Disappointments, if not recognized, handled and overcome will damage, mangle and mismanage our potential to become a person who breaks through the wall of our disenchanted times and experiences. Disappointments can damage the soul's reaction to the presence of God. It damages the heart's reaction to the presence of others around us. It damages the mind and emotional reaction to ourselves and violates our vision of the world in which we live. Perhaps the answer is, to disappoint our disappointments and let them know that it has no charge over our lives.

I guess the thing to do is, to get a grip on our disappointments before they get a grip on us.

SCRIPTURE FOR MEDITATION

Do not cast me from your presence or take your Holy Spirit from me. Restore to me the joy of your salvation and grant me a willing spirit, to sustain me.

Psalm 51:11-12

PRAYER

Lord, I am often broken by disappointments. My pillow is often wet with tears because of my disappointments. My friends have let me down. My family seems to forget me. The world disappoints me. I am more disappointed than I am happy and made glad. Lord, show me how to take charge over my disappointments and not allow them to have charge over me. I will forever rejoice in your peace. Amen.

Personal Journal Thoughts:

How do you view disappoints? How can you use your disappointments to build your future?

Bouncing Back From Disappointments

God will not permit any trouble to come upon us, unless He has a specific plan by which great blessing can come out of the difficulty.

PETER MARSHALL

One of the hardest lessons to learn is how to bounce back from disappointments. Bouncing back from disappointing experiences whether it is disappointment in us, or in others, is not accomplished automatically. We bounce back from disappointments by making a deliberate choice not to allow them to put our lives under arrest. I've discovered that when we make up our minds and find the courage to bounce back from our disappointments, we will discover that we have been given the power to get over anything, no matter the severity of the pain.

It's imperative to keep bouncing back regardless of how deep our disappointments may be, because it is during disappointments when the enemy seeks to steal our bounce. We must remember not to allow the enemy to steal our ability to bounce back. Therefore, pressing beyond our disappointments must be a deliberate and conscious act on our part and if we do this, God will do the rest.

SCRIPTURE FOR MEDITATION

Do not let your heart be troubled. Trust in God; trust also in me.

John 14:1

PRAYER

Dear heavenly Father, hear my prayer. Many are my disappointments that I don't always understand. But, regardless of my disappointments I trust you for strength to rise above my disappointing moments. Increase my faith in order that I may bounce back from those things that have brought me disappointments and pain. Amen.

My Personal Journal Thoughts: *What can you do in order to bounce back from your disappointments?*

Personal Journal Thoughts:

How do you view disappoints? How can you use your disappointments to build your future?

 ## In God's Awesomeness

Wonder is the attitude of admiration for life's beauty, perfection, and subtlety. Wonder is the attitude of awe in the presence of life's vastness and power. Wonder is the attitude of reverence for the infinite values and meanings of life, and of marveling over God's purpose and patience in it all. Thus wonder leads to the birth of constructive imagination and vision, and soon issues in the more triumphant verbs I see and I believe.

GEORGE WALTER FISKE

The depth of the awesomeness of God is usually hard to explain, if it can be explained at all. Perhaps it is not ours to give explanation to such wonder, but to simply enjoy and respond. Each day offers seconds, minutes and hours to come into the awesomeness of the Infinite by which we are refreshed.

To come into the Creator's awesomeness is to acknowledge that He is most powerful in all that He performs. We cannot come into the presence of the Almighty and leave without truly acknowledging that His existence is beyond the finite minds of man. Secondly, to come into God's awesomeness is to allow ourselves to be overtaken by His divine presence, even if we don't understand it all. It is sometimes in us not knowing all we desire to know about Him when we come into a new knowledge of His unlimited power. Thirdly, to come into the awesome presence of the Creator, is to live our lives empowered by His presence by which we are given the energy to change things and to alter our lives.

When these are accomplished, then we shall come into His awesome presence where we are challenged to encounter life head-on without the weight of fear. It is when we come into His awesome presence, the awful encounters we sometimes are faced with are overtaken by His glory and we are given the courage to keep moving forward.

SCRIPTURE FOR MEDITATION

In your majesty ride forth victoriously in behalf of truth, humility and righteousness; let your right hand display awesome deeds.

Psalm 45:4

PRAYER

Lord, I offer to you glory and praise! You are awesome in all you do. Had it not been for your mighty hand upon me the problems of life would have consumed me. But, your awesome graces, kindness, love and mercy has kept me all the day. Glory to your awesome name! Amen.

Personal Journal Thoughts:

How do you view the awesomeness of God's presence in your life? What does it mean to you?

_____
_____
_____
_____
_____
_____
_____
_____
_____
_____
_____
_____
_____
_____
_____
_____
_____
_____
_____
_____
_____
_____
_____

 Becoming a New Creation

To give life a meaning one must have a purpose larger than one's self.

WILL DURANT

There are times when our days start like the first day of the creation of the earth – empty, dark and void. Sometimes the day starts in some type of chaos – turning and moving, and spinning in many directions and ways with no compass. The directions are not always easy to identify, and we cannot always understand the way in which we are going. This is the very time we need God – the Creator to speak as He did in the beginning when nothing existed but emptiness, darkness and void.

It's only when we allow God to speak to our world, whatever condition it is in and we heed to what He says, it is then our world changes and flourishes in becoming something better than before.

God hasn't changed; He is still the Creator who speaks things into existence.

When God speaks – when He says let there be, all that He commands to be – becomes. When God speaks things come to order. That which did not exist becomes that which never was. Our lives become full of energy, sound and light when God speaks, in spite of the darkness and the chaos that sometimes exists.

When we allow God to speak to our world and we take heed to His voice, then our world is determined by what He says and we find the right direction in which we should go, if we would simply hear and follow Him.

In a world filled with so many voices speaking into our ears and minds, it is most imperative to listen for the unique voice of the Creator who gives us direction. If our world is going to change and flourish with newness, it has to start with "God said".

SCRIPTURE FOR MEDITATION

For you created my inmost being; you knit me together in my mother's womb ... I am fearfully and wonderfully made; your works are wonderful ... My frame was not hidden from you when I was made ... When I was woven together ... your eyes saw my unformed body. All the days ordained for me were written in your book before one of them came to be.

Psalm 139:13-16

PRAYER

Dear heavenly Father, thank you for all the new things you do for me, even when I am under arrest by my past. Thank you for making me afresh by the power of your mighty hands. Create in me a clean heart and renew a right spirit within me. Take the old me and reshape it into something great and new for your glory. Amen!

Personal Journal Thoughts:

As God speaks to you, how do you picture yourself in the present and in the future? Envision the new you!

 When Deep Calls To Deep

To us also, through every star, through every blade of grass, is not God made visible if we will open our minds and eyes?
THOMAS CARLYLE

There are days when we awake facing dilemmas, decisions, temptations, challenges, changes and most of all ourselves, and we wonder how to deal with such pressures. Unfortunately, there seems to be no ready answers on the surface of our search for clarity in moments such as these. It's possible that these encounters call us towards a deeper search for clarity. This is when deep calls for deep, whatever that depth is.

Each of us have some deep place that we dare not expose to the world around us, least we are judged by the shallow. This is the deep where no one exits but us and God.

Deep! Depth! They call to the other!

Deep is God Himself. God is deep. There is no person who has mastered the deep besides God. He is deepest, as far as deep can go. It is He who calls for a meeting between us and Himself along with our dilemmas in life whatever they may be, to give us direction on how to move from the surface of life towards a new depth of Him, ourselves and the things we encounter.

When we allow ourselves to be drawn into deeper experiences with God we find something deep about life, and that is that life is full of un-chartered waters, full of new and fresh experiences that adds to life.

The deep calls for depth. Deep challenges us to view life from a different perspective. It demands that we move from the surface of things to the deeper meaning of life experiences. When we dare go deeper we see more of God, more about ourselves and more about the world around us.

Even in the darkest abyss, we can see the light, for God is there.

SCRIPTURE FOR MEDIATION

Deep calls to deep in the roar of your waterfalls; all your waves and breakers have swept over me. By day the Lord directs his love, at night his song is with me – a prayer to the God of my life.
Psalm 42:7-8

PRAYER

Lord, there is no measuring your awesome depth. My mind cannot conceive the depth of your presence. Your power I cannot understand and your mercy over shadow me. Your grace and mercy shines in darkness and I am moved to praise your divine depth. Lord, take me deeper into your presence in order that I may be made whole. Amen.

Personal Journal Thoughts:

As you listen to God's voice call you into deeper experiences with Him, how will you respond? What will your life look like if you heed to God's voice to move beyond the meaningless and the mundane?

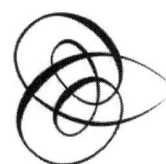 # Going Beyond Contentment

True contentment is the power of getting out of any situation all that there is in it.

GILBERT KEITH CHESTERTON

We are sometimes tempted to take the easiest road we can find and become complacent with average – just barely making it – simply surviving from one day to the other, never attempting to raise to new and higher levels. This is a dangerous point to be at in life.

Ours is the choice to remain where we are in life or attempt to move to the next level. If we remain where we are, even though we are alive we can be dead inwardly. If we move to the next level, we live and God receives the glory, and those around us will be blessed and encouraged by our successes as we are encouraged to do greater things.

The greatest battle many of us are faced with is not particularly the world around us, or the troubles we are sometimes confronted with. But, the greatest battle we face is us becoming wrongfully content. Being wrongfully content is to become satisfied with what we have been successful at when we have the ability and potential to accomplish more

We should learn to deal with our situations until our change comes and do what we can do at the moment in order to move forward and use our abilities and potential to help bring such change into reality. If we simply wait for something to happen – for something to change, it will not occur due to our wrongful contentment. Things happen and things change in time, but we must work at planning for our future. A good and productive future doesn't become reality simply by dreaming of a great future. A good and productive future is manifest in our present when we plan for it and work at it.

God forbid if we should spend the rest of our lives in places that yield no harvest. Perhaps we are all guilty of burying our talents under the rubbish of wrongful contentment – simply waiting with no real efforts and expectation for the future.

SCRIPTURE FOR MEDITATION

... I press on to take hold of that for which Christ Jesus took hold of me... I do not consider myself yet to have taken hold of it. But one thing I do: Forgetting what is behind and straining toward what is ahead.
Philippians 3:12-13

PRAYER

Dear heavenly Father, thank you for my life. You have created me with purpose and have given me the power and the ability to change things around me. Let me not become wrongfully content with life the way it is, when I can do more. Teach me not to stand still when I should be moving forward. Direct me in your way and will for my life in order that I may use every gift and ability you have given me, in order to lift up your great name and bless others. Amen.

Personal Journal Thoughts:

What plans do you have for your future? What do you intend to do about it?

# We Are That Place

You can within yourself find a mighty, unexplored kingdom in which you can dwell in peace if you will.

RUSSELL H. CONWELL

Oftentimes we meet the day not knowing what is ahead. There are times when we go about our routine not really expecting God to show His presence in some awesome way and manner. It's often in the unexpected places when we are affirmed by God's presence and confirmed by His power. God sometimes allow us to stumble into the kingdom realm where He captures us in the midst of an anointing move. We are caught by surprise and the only sensible or humanly thing to do is to surrender.

There are times when God move and take us to places that is out of this world – no description – no definition of the moment – no song written for it and no book written about it. It's all new! It is that place where we are refreshed and renewed and energized by His powerful presence and by the sound of His voice. In this place our dreams and visions are confirmed. The place of which I speak we cannot name at times. But, we know that it exists and the only way we arrive there is that we learn to sometimes move through life without programs and agendas – no plans at the moment – just ready and open to God.

Many of us have gone to this place many times. It exists, because we were there. We heard God's voice so clearly. We don't want Him to stop speaking to us. It's real, because we were there in this place from our birth. We felt His hand upon us. At times we wondered where this place was we had journeyed to. To our amazement we discovered that this place was in us. For, the kingdom of God is in us. The place we had entered was in us and we discovered more of ourselves and more of God. We are that place where we meet God and He is in the place with us.

We should never want to leave this place in which we've arrived. For in a world so fake, this place is real.

SCRIPTURE FOR MEDITATION

Search me, O God, and know my heart; test me and know my anxious thoughts. See if there is any offensive way in me, and lead me in the way everlasting.

Psalm 139:23-24

PRAYER

Lord, thank you for creating me. Thank you for making me who I am. I do not take my life for granted. I am blessed with life. Show me how to be all you have made me. Teach me how to acknowledge my weaknesses and my strengths. Most of all teach me to be me. Amen.

Personal Journal Thoughts:

Where are you with God? What is God saying to you? How will you respond to Him?

Dealing with Giants, Battles, Fears and Failures

Do not pray for easy lives; pray to be stronger men. Do not pray for task equal to your powers; pray for powers equal to your task. Then the doing of your work shall be no miracle, but you shall be a miracle. Every day you shall wonder at yourself, at the richness of life which comes to you by the grace of God.
PHILLIP BROOKS

It is interesting that we spend our time facing and fighting the same giants, battles, fears and failures we fought and faced the previous day. We often face the same dreadful things each morning. Perhaps this is due to some fault and error of our own, due to us overlooking the urgency of subduing those things that prevented us from moving forward yesterday.

If we fail to conquer and overcome our giants, battles, fears and failures or at least put forth an honest effort to deal with them, we will face them the next day. When we fail to deal with the things we should deal with in the present, tomorrow becomes basically like reruns of old cinema flicks, outdated, and uneventful because we know how the story ends. Our future becomes colorless like old black and white movies fading with time and with poor sound.

We must put forth a determined effort to change the script of our lives by overcoming, subduing and being victorious over the negatives in our present least we spend the rest of lives in repeat which soon becomes bland and boring.

We must be determined to face our obstacles now, or face them tomorrow. And as we stand firm in our faith, we should remember that as we face our giants, battles, fears and failures, we have a very present help – God Almighty.

SCRIPTURE FOR MEDITATION

The Lord is my light and my salvation – whom shall I fear? The Lord is the stronghold of my life – of whom shall I be afraid? When evil men advance against me to devour my flesh, when my enemies and my foes attack me, they will stumble and fall. Though an army besiege me, my heart will not fear; though war break out against me, even then will I be confident.

Psalm 27:1-3

PRAYER

Dear heavenly Father, there are times when I am faced with the giants of life that sometimes cause me to fear. There are times when I am weak in the shadows of my giants and I lose the battle. Sometimes my fears get the best of me and I fail in my faith. Teach me Oh Lord to trust you no matter what I face. For I know that your presence is always with me. Amen.

Personal Journal Thoughts:

What are your giants, battles, fears and failures and how do you deal with them? What can you do to win over the obstacles that stand in the way of your success?

Facing Mountains and Valleys

I saw the mountains stand Silent, wonderful, and grand, Looking across the land When the golden light was falling On distant dome and spire; And I heard a low voice calling, "Come up higher, come up higher," From the lowlands and the mire, From the mist of earth's desire, From the vain pursuit of pelf, From the attitude of self: "Come up higher, come up higher.

JAMES S. CLARK

In life we are presented with two options that make the difference of how our future turns out. This depends on the choices we make: Mountains or Valleys? Which do we choose? God will not make this choice for us neither can those around us make the choice for us. If we do nothing, it's a choice. If we do something it is still a choice. But, it is a matter of our choosing which route we will go – Mountains or Valleys?

Personal Journal Thoughts:

How do you view the mountains and valleys in your life? What route do you plan to take and how will you do it?

# Resilience

The human capacity for burden is like bamboo – far more flexible than you'd ever believe at first glance.

Jodi Picoult

Resilience! A common definition of resilience is something having the ability to bounce or spring back into shape or position. It is the ability to recover strength, spirit, and good humor – buoyancy.

My personal definition of resilience is someone having the ability or even the faith and courage to bounce or spring back into their original shape, form and position after being twisted or bent over by certain situations. It is one's refusal to stay on the bottom when the pressure of life presses in on them. It's having the faith and boldness in the strength of God, to keep springing back into shape when we have been bent out of shape and torn. Resilience gives us the power to bounce back into position in spite of our disappointments, and sometimes having the strength to laugh about it.

Resiliency is to be buoyant. It's having the determination to float back to the surface when we have been weighed down by some unfortunate encounter. It's our ability to ride and float on the ripples of life.

Finally, resilience is having the faith and the ability to take the chance to try something again that we failed at before or to attempt something different even if it bends us out of shape or out of our comfort zone, while knowing that God is in total control of our destiny and will not allow us to be bent beyond our ability to bounce to back.

SCRIPTURE FOR MEDITATION

Be on your guard; stand firm in the faith; be men of courage; be strong.

1 Corinthians 16:13

PRAYER

Dear heavenly Father, give me the power and the courage to bounce back when I have been weighed down by the concerns of this world. Teach me to keep moving forward regardless of the circumstances I face. Amen.

Personal Journal Thoughts:

What bend you out of shape? What steps can you take in order to bounce back from the things that cause you to be bent out of shape?

_____
_____
_____
_____
_____
_____
_____
_____
_____
_____
_____
_____
_____
_____
_____
_____
_____
_____
_____
_____
_____
_____
_____
_____

 *Getting Reconnected*

The spirit of man is stronger than anything that can happen to it.

ROBERT FALCON SCOTT

Working long hours, making deals, meeting deadlines, fast cars, hectic schedules, car horns going off, sirens blazing, babies crying, dogs barking – red lights, yellow lights and nobody slowing down – green lights and people are standing still – people moving too fast and going nowhere or not moving fast enough or not at all – just disconnected!

Life can be composed of one disconnection after another!

If one is not careful to remember the importance of staying connected to the things that make life work, we can become disconnected from reality and life moves with very little meaning and purpose. I mean things like – those moments that make us smile and laugh in rough times – family love – true friendships – sun shine beaming through the window in the morning – birds singing after a stormy night – the sound of mellow chimes dancing in a gentle breeze at sunset – children laughing in the backyard – the smell of fresh brewed coffee in the morning – the smell of chicken frying in the kitchen – being able to stay in bed on a chilly Saturday morning or just simple silence after a hard day's work, but most of all, feeling God's gentle breath blowing life in to our lungs just because He loves us. It's worth getting reconnected.

SCRIPTURE FOR MEDITATION

Let us draw near to God with a sincere heart in full assurance of faith, having our hearts sprinkled to cleanse us from a guilty conscience and having our bodies washed with pure water. Let us hold unswervingly to the hope we profess, for he who promised is faithful.

Hebrews 12:22-23

PRAYER

Lord, there are days when I feel so far from you. There are days when I am so human and weak that I am unable to come to you. Have mercy on me. Extend your grace to me so that I may come unto you and be restored. Forgive me for being away for so long. Heal me in order that I may stand firm in your Holy presence. Reconnect me to your divine power. Amen.

Personal Journal Thoughts:

How's your connection with God? How can you become more connected with God's presence?

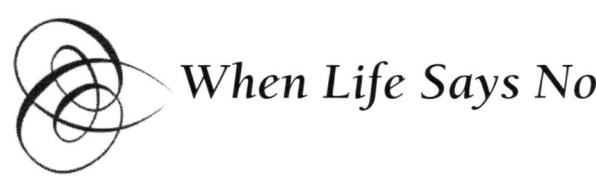 # When Life Says No

A possibility is a hint from God. One must follow it. In every man there is latent the highest possibility.

SOREN KIERKEGAARD

Life presents us with the one word we prefer not to hear and that is the word "No", even though it is necessary at times. Each of us gets a "No" from time to time. Some of our greatest breakthroughs have come at the heel of us being told "No".

"No" is a needed ingredient for success in some cases. However, when "No" comes at a time when we have put forth our best efforts to reach and grab our dream – when we have been promised a "Yes" to our dreams, visions, efforts and desires – "No" can be unacceptable.

When we have done our best to stay positive and to offer something positive to society – "No" to our progress is an unacceptable response. But, what should our response be when life presents us with a "No" instead of a "Yes" to our dreams, prayers, ideas, visions and our best efforts?

When faced with a "No" after we have done our best, we should keep pressing our faith until we transform our "No" into a "Yes".

We cannot take "No's" in life and simply live by them if we are going to reach some pinnacle of success. Faith doesn't allow us to set back and allow "No" to have complete control of our destiny and purpose. Faith demands that "No" changes into "Yes". After all nothing is impossible for those of us who trust in God who have promised to answer our prayers according to His will.

SCRIPTURE FOR MEDITATION

… According to your faith will it be done to you.

Matthew 9:29

PRAYER

Dear heavenly Father, thank you for life and health. As I travel through life I am sometimes confronted with "No". I know that there are some things that are not meant for me. Help me know the difference between my "yes" and my "no". Help me to identify those things that are for me and have the courage to take hold of them without fear. Give me the wisdom not to spend time on those things that are not meant for me. For I know that in your plan when life says "No", you have something greater for me. Amen.

Personal Journal Thoughts:

When the world says "No" to your dreams how can you turn it into "Yes"?

_____
_____
_____
_____
_____
_____
_____
_____
_____
_____
_____
_____
_____
_____
_____
_____
_____
_____
_____
_____
_____
_____
_____

 *In Pursuit Of Happiness*

Such happiness as life is capable of comes from the full participation of all our powers in the endeavor to wrest from each changing situation of experiences its own full and unique meaning.

JOHN DEWEY

One of the greatest quests in life is that of the pursuit of happiness. Being happy is not automatic. Perhaps happiness was somewhat automatic when we were children. When we had no real concerns and life was free and easy. But, once we crossed the threshold into adulthood happiness seem to have gotten lost amongst our hurried days – rush hour traffic – paying bills, raising children, helping with homework, or just simply trying to survive in this crazy world.

True happiness is something we take hold of deliberately. It is not by accident that we take hold of happiness. It's by choice. Happiness is a state of mind and soul. It's a state of our insight and deep positive feelings about life that is not based upon the accumulation of things. Happiness is taken hold of when we hunt for it and make it our aim and our business. The question is; how do we pursue happiness and grab it?

I offer the following as it relate to taking hold of happiness and making it our own:

- Make God's presence your first pursuit. He is the root of our happiness.
- Take time to settle down and rest in happy thoughts, no matter how tough things are.
- Realize that your problems are seasonal. Trouble don't last always.
- Realize that your happiness comes from within versus without. Don't depend on others to determine your happiness.
- Surround yourself with those who want you to be happy and are pursuers of happiness themselves. We can't make our company with those who prefer darkness over light and expect to be happy.
- Don't depend on material things or even money to make you happy. Money can't buy happiness and things cannot assure us joy.
- Learn to laugh even when you don't feel like it. Laughing has the power to make us happy in the toughest of times.

Finally, each morning you wake up, pause and thank God for another day, for being alive is enough to be happy about.

SCRIPTURE FOR MEDITATION

I know that there is nothing better for men than to be happy and do good while they live ... and find satisfaction in all his toil – this is the gift of God. I know that everything God does will endure forever; nothing can be added to it and nothing taken from it ...

Ecclesiastes 3:12-14

PRAYER

Lord, thank you for happy moments, even in the midst of troubled times. Teach me to pursue happiness no matter how rough and though life gets. My true happiness is found in you when I trust you and remember your promises. Guide me each day in a pursuit of happiness in order that my life may be a light to others. Amen.

Personal Journal Thoughts:

Take the time and record the things that make you happy. What can you do to assure that you live a happy life in spite of your difficulties?

_____
_____
_____
_____
_____
_____
_____
_____
_____
_____
_____
_____
_____
_____
_____
_____
_____
_____
_____
_____
_____
_____
_____
_____

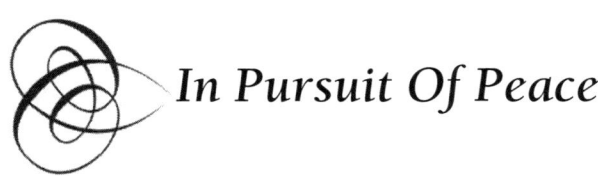
In Pursuit Of Peace

But all the pleasures that I find Is to maintain a quiet mind.

EDWARD DYER

Finding peace is not easy in a time like this that constantly warrants our attention and time. We live in a rush and hurried time – no time to relax – no time to think clearly (many of us operate our lives with undeveloped thoughts) - we are always moving about – can't keep still – bombarded by the tensions of the day and the stresses of the next day – still tripping about our past with no hope for tomorrow. As a result of such issues painting our lives with dark colored hues, we fail to grasp one of the most important ingredients that help paint our lives brighter and that is – Peace!

Peace can truly be found in God and our relationship with Him. When we are connected to God by seeking to be in His presence, He gives us His peace in spite of our storms. In order to establish a life full of God's peace we should do the following:

- Pursue God daily.
- Don't depend on the actions of others to bring you peace even though they play an important role in our lives.
- Slow down long enough to smell the flowers.
- Talk to God more than you talk to people.

- Remember that those who create peace and give peace to others; will have peace within themselves. For we reap what we plant.

Peace – Free from war – an undisturbed state of mind – a sense of calmness – a state of tranquility – an ordered life.

SCRIPTURE FOR MEDITATION

The fruit of righteousness will be peace; the effect of righteousness will be quietness and confidence forever.

Isaiah 32:17

PRAYER

Dear heavenly Father, life is sometimes made up of storms that come to steal my peace. Restore my peace in your divine presence. When the waves of life, beat upon me teach me to be calm under your mighty wings. Amen.

Personal Journal Thoughts:

Take the time to record the things that brings you peace. How can you make your life more peaceful?

_____
_____
_____
_____
_____
_____
_____
_____
_____
_____
_____
_____
_____
_____
_____
_____
_____
_____
_____
_____
_____
_____
_____
_____

 Fulfilling Your Destiny

We and God must have business one with the other and in opening our hearts to Him our highest destiny is fulfilled.

WILLIAM JAMES

We all have a destiny that is designed by God. Our destiny is only reached when we do our best to reach it. We do not reach our destiny simply because we wake up in the morning and wish for it. It takes determination, focus, discipline, prayer and faith in God.

In reaching our destiny the following 7 principles apply:

1) Don't tolerate those things that hinder you from going forward. What we tolerate will not change on its own instead it usually changes us. 2) When you are going for that for which you are created, remember that smallness will ring out. Greatness forces smallness to cry out. Pay no attention to it. 3) When you are going for your destiny, logic will collide with faith, only we can determine which one wins.
4) Remember we reach our destiny in pieces. We must take one step at a time. Patience is a must when attempting to reach our

destiny. 5) Be who God has made you and not who others want you to be. People did not create you, so don't allow them to mold you into who they want you to be. Be you, for only you can reach your destiny. 6) Remember that if you stay the course that leads to your destiny, you will end up running into the resources you need to reach it. Therefore, take nothing or any person for granted. 7) As you pursue your destiny have courage even when you are not encouraged to keep moving forward. Keep facing forward in order to see where you are and where you are going.

You are closer to your destiny than you realize. For no man can keep moving in the right direction of his destiny and not get closer to it. This is a law of nature.

SCRIPTURE FOR MEDITATION

For I know the plans I have for you, declares the Lord, "plans to prosper you and not to harm you, plans to give you hope and a future. Then you will call upon me and come to me, and I will listen to you. You will seek me with all your heart. I will be found by you," declares the Lord...
Jeremiah 29:11-14

PRAYER

Lord, thank you for giving me a purpose to live. I am not an accident of nature. You purposefully created me to do great and wonderful works for your glory and for helping others. You have given me a destiny. Guide me to the place for which I am created without fear. Let nothing stand between me and the destiny for which I am created. Amen.

Personal Journal Thoughts:

How do you see your destiny? What are your goals that will lead you to your destiny?

Divine Providence

To have striven, to have made an effort, to have been true to certain ideas – this alone is worth the struggle. We are here to add what we can to, not to get what we can from, life.

WILLIAM OSLER

Life moves with rhythm, and that rhythm flows in the river of Divine Providence – the Providential River. Divine Providence is God's way of getting us to the place where our lives are fulfilled. It's His powerful guidance that pushes us closer to that for which we are deliberately created. No person exists by accident or mishap – God controls all things. Divine providence had a hand in it. We are all born with a purpose and for a purpose. We are pushed and pulled towards our purpose by God's hand through various circumstances and experiences, whether they are positive or negative. Nothing in life happens by happenstance or by some coincidence – but by providence.

Each person we meet can add something to us that gets us closer to who we are designed to be, whether that person is negative or positive.

Pains, heartaches, disappointments, moments of discouragement, successes, failures, mistakes or losses does not occur in our lives to stop us from reaching the pinnacles of success, but each experience is designed and controlled by God in order to push and pull us farther down the providential river, if we would trust Him and not jump overboard. Then we will reach the port of our purpose, knowing that it was God's hand that guided us along the ripples.

SCRIPTURE FOR MEDITATION

And we know that in all things God works for the good of those who love him, who have been called according to his purpose.

Romans 8:28

PRAYER

Dear heavenly Father, thank you for every event and experience in my life. Some are negative and some are positive. Some make me laugh, while others make me cry. But, I thank you for each experience. I know that all things are working together for my good and that nothing is out of your control. Teach me how to trust you in every experience in my life. Build my faith when I become afraid. Amen.

Personal Journal Thoughts:

How do you view your experiences in light of God's control?

Waiting for Something Worthwhile

The art of waiting is not learned at once. The child must wait until he is old enough to have a bicycle, the young man until he is old enough to drive a car, the medical student must wait for his diploma, the young couple for saving for a new home.

HOWARD WHITMAN

In order for life to yield its best, we must discover something in life that is worth waiting for until it comes. We do not reach the peaks in life until we have learned the art of waiting – the lesson of patience in the classroom of some valley, as we sit in deep expectation for something we deeply believe in to happen.

If we do not discover a dream, a task, a project or some passion that drives us to wait for it, and is worth fighting the temptation of quitting, we discover that we will never reach the peaks in life and our lives becomes mundane and uneventful.

In order for life to be fulfilling, we must search through the rubbish of our journey and discover something so deep – something so powerful – something that is unexplainable in logical words that drives us to fight for it – to wait patiently for it, until life yields every dream – every hope – every idea and every great expectation. Then we will find ourselves on the peak of some success, knowing that we have waited as we were determined to get to the top.

SCRIPTURE FOR MEDITATION

...Write down the revelation and make it plan ... For the revelation awaits an appointed time... and will not prove false. Though it linger, wait for it; it will certainly come and will not delay.

Habakkuk 2:2-3

PRAYER

Lord, teach me to wait. Waiting is not an easy task to perform in times like these. But, I know that all things are in your hand that concerns me. Therefore, I shall wait until my change comes. For in you I put my trust. Keep me calm as I wait for your deliverance and favor. Amen

Personal Journal Thoughts:

What do you expect out of life? What will you do in order to see your expectations become reality?

 ## Overcoming Life's Obstacles

Faith that obstacles could be surmounted made men and women venture upon the seas, dare the wilderness, cross the rivers, the plains, the Rockies, and the High Sierras to open up America.

FLORENCE E. ALLEN

Every obstacle in life can be overcome, and great and lasting success can be achieved by hard work and focused faith and with a determined purpose. We overcome the various obstacles we face in life when we work hard at reaching the pinnacles of our successes without quitting.

We reach the pinnacles of our success when we keep our faith focused on what we expect to receive out of life in the face of obstacles of any kind, and we accompany our faith with a determined purpose. A determined purpose; is to have the courage to press through obstacles with a particular aim in mind and not allow anything or anybody to turn us from the ultimate purpose for which we are created.

SCRIPTURE FOR MEDITATION

Now faith is being sure of what we hope for and certain of what we do not see.
Hebrews 11:1

PRAYER

Dear heavenly Father, many are the obstacles that stand in my way to keep me from your blessings and favor and to keep me from the destiny that you have purposed for me. Give me the wisdom and strength to press beyond those things that stands against me in order that I may give you full glory and that my life will be a light to others. Amen.

Personal Journal Thoughts:

What do you believe is the purpose of your life? What can you do in order to live within your purpose?

# Pressing On Anyhow

The only limit to our realization of tomorrow will be our doubt of today. Let us move forward with strong and active faith.

FRANKLIN D. ROOSEVELT

Sometimes we start in a certain direction; only to be slowed down by some obstacle, temptation, and problem, or fear of something, or some mistake or failure. I guess the human thing to do is to stop in our tracks instead of pressing on. It's easier to give into our problems.

When we are faced with problems and obstacles that challenge our courage to keep moving forward, we must make up our minds to press on anyhow – In spite of.

To press on anyhow is to keep moving forward regardless of the walls we face.

To press on anyhow, is to keep the faith regardless of what we see or don't see, knowing that faith is the substance of the things we hope for and the evidence of the things we do not see with the natural eye and the evidence of our dreams that has yet to become reality.

To press on anyhow, is to attempt the seemingly impossible, while knowing that all things are possible through Christ who is our strength.

To press on anyhow, is to keep moving in the direction of our purpose and destiny in spite of our failures, knowing that our failures are not final – they are just pauses in our progression.

To press on anyhow, is to challenge our odds more than they challenge us.

SCRIPTURE FOR MEDITATION

And the God of all grace, who called you to his eternal glory in Christ, after you have suffered a little while, will himself restore you and make you strong, firm and steadfast.

1 Peter 5:10

PRAYER

Lord, I offer to you glory and praise for all you have done, even when I am faced with challenges. There are times when I feel defeated and too weak to press on, but through your divine power I am empowered to keep going. Give me the boldness to press through my challenges regardless of how tough things get. Amen.

Personal Journal Thoughts:

How do you view the obstacles in your life and what can you do to develop a faith that empowers you to press on anyhow?

_____
_____
_____
_____
_____
_____
_____
_____
_____
_____
_____
_____
_____
_____
_____
_____
_____
_____
_____
_____
_____
_____
_____
_____
_____

# Keeping Balance

The steps of faith fall on the seeming void and find the rock beneath.

WALT WHITMAN

We can sometimes get off balance. Life can be one balancing act after another. Keeping balance is a must if we are going to live affective and successful lives. Maintaining balance must be a priority if we expect our lives to yield its best fruit.

How to maintain balance:

- In order to maintain balance, we should keep our minds and hearts focused on our purpose for being alive. We should not give our attention to those things that do not matter.
- In order to maintain balance, we should build our lives on pure principles, standards and morals that add to the good of humanity. Pure principles, standards and morals keep us in the middle and from going over the edge.
- In order to maintain balance, discipline is a major ingredient for stability. Without discipline we give ourselves to the things that do not help us in becoming

all we can become. When we live beneath who we are created to be, life get's off balance.
- In order to maintain balance, we must be true to ourselves as much as possible. By acknowledging who we are – our weaknesses and strengths, we are then equipped to combat the temptations and fears that sometimes throw us off balance.
- In order to maintain balance, keeping the faith is a major key to stability. We must believe that through Christ all things are possible even when we are walking a tight rope in the wind.

SCRIPTURE FOR MEDITATION

It is God who arms me with strength and makes my way perfect. He makes my feet like the feet of a deer; he enables me to stand on the heights.

Psalm 18:32-33

PRAYER

Dear heavenly Father, I confess that I sometimes lose my balance in life and slip from your ways. Teach me how to keep my balance in this slippery world in order that I may bring you glory and benefit from your divine favor. Amen.

Personal Journal Thoughts:

What does it mean to have a balanced life and how can you maintain your balance?

 # Playing the Cards You Are Dealt

Faith is an act of rational choice which determines us to act as if certain things were true and in the confident expectation that they will prove to be true.

WILLIAM RALPH INGE

Each person born into this world is dealt a hand of cards we did not ask for. Some are good and others not so good. It is not the hand we are dealt that makes the biggest difference. It's how we play the hand we are dealt.

We are granted the option to attempt to play the cards we are dealt in life or let the cards play us. Either way the cards will be played. We can play them or sit back and fold. If we simply sit back and fold without putting forth an effort to win the game, we will surely lose. However, if we at least attempt to play the hand we are dealt whether it is good or bad, our chances of winning the game is most probable. At least we have put forth the effort to stay in the game until the next hand is dealt.

It is not always the cards we are dealt in life, whether they look promising or not, it's how we attempt to play them. This I have learned throughout the years.

Whatever we do – we cannot fold simply because the hand we are dealt doesn't look promising. After all, every hand we are dealt has a purpose and since God is the Major Dealer – the hand we are dealt is all for our good, whether we agree with it or not. So, we should stay in the game and not fold or quit before time. For quitting should never be an option we entertain. Folding in the game is not an option for winners and the faithful.

SCRIPTURE FOR MEDITATION

Trust in the Lord with all your heart and lean not on your own understanding; in all your ways acknowledge him, and he will make your paths straight. Do not be wise in your own eyes; fear the Lord and shun evil. This will bring health to your body and nourishment to your bones.

Proverbs 3:5-8

PRAYER

Lord, thank you for every episode of my life. I confess that I don't always agree with everything that happens in my life. But, your mercy and your grace sustain me when I don't understand. I believe that you are in control of every event that takes place in my life. I believe that every card that is dealt in my life is under your divine control. Teach me to be still until my change come. Amen.

Personal Journal Thoughts:

How do you view your life? Do you see your life as a bad deal? What can you do change a bad deal into a good hand?

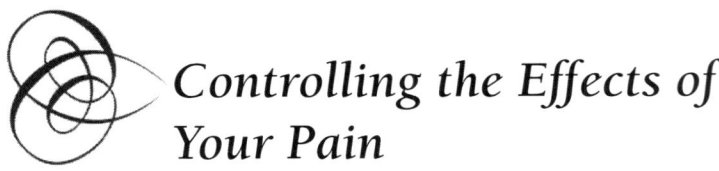
Controlling the Effects of Your Pain

The pessimist sees the difficulty in every opportunity; the optimist, the opportunity in every difficulty.

L. P. JACKS

We all experience pain at some point or another. Sometimes the pain we encounter is imposed upon us by those close to us, as well as by those who are not so close. Some of our painful encounters are self-imposed. We hurt ourselves at times.

Sometimes our pain occurs by the natural flow of life. Pain is an inevitable encounter that we all face. Whether it is imposed upon us by the hands of others or by our own hands or by natural occurrences, we have control over the effect our pain have on us.

We may not always be able to control exactly how our pain occurs or what form it comes in, but we can control the effect it has on the rest of our life. Either we can allow our pain to stop us in our tracks or we can use such experiences to push us over the top. This is a matter of choice we are all granted through God's power.

SCRIPTURE FOR MEDITATION

Though he slay me, yet will I hope in him...

Job 13:15

PRAYER

Dear heavenly Father, great is your name in all the earth! I praise you Father for the power you have given me to stand firm in my storms. You have made me strong by your divine power. Teach me to deal with every experience I encounter as I rest in your divine presence and providence. Amen.

Personal Journal Thoughts:

How can you be successful in spite of the pain you have experienced?

 Taking Hold of the New

The present is always determined by the past, and always we are free to determine the future.

H. J. FORMAN

Look around you and you will see that things are changing. God is doing a new thing regardless of the way things look!

Time is moving on. If we are to live full and empowered lives in the days to come, we must take hold of the new that is being exposed in the now. In order to take hold of the new, we must do our best to release the negative experiences of our past, as well as the negative episodes that is present in our lives today. It is important that we do our best to release our negative past, because if we allow our negatives past to control our present, we live in defeat. Regardless of what has occurred in our past or even taking place presently, we must keep pushing forward towards the new. We must ask God for the power to let go of those things and even people that keeps us from taking hold of the new. Then we will be able to take hold the new abundance that God has for us.

In order to take hold of the new that God provides, we have to let go of our old selves and outdated ways. Now is the time for the new!

SCRIPTURE FOR MEDITATION

Forget the former things ... I am doing a new thing ... Now it springs up ... I am making away in the desert ...
Isaiah 43:18-19

PRAYER

Lord, awesome is the power of your hands. My eyes behold the splendor of your divine power. You are the Creator of all things. Thank you God for another day! Guide me by your mighty hand beyond my past and into the future for which you have purposed me. Teach me how not to take my days for granted, for each day is a gift from you. Amen.

Personal Journal Thoughts:

How do you view each day you are given and what can you do to make the best of it? What is your new?

 # The Power of Your Mind

Your living is determined not so much by what life brings to you as by the attitude you bring to life; not so much by what happens to you as by the way your mind looks at what happens.

KHALIL GIBRAN

A man's feet will only go as far as his mind. We will never go farther than our minds will imagine. We only attempt those things we have perceived in our minds. Our mind is the garden of our activities.

What we do or attempt to do is the sum total of that which has grown in our minds whether we attempt the negative or the positive, something small or great, or something forgettable or worth remembering. It all starts in the mind. Our lives are only as healthy as our minds are.

We must spend time filling our minds with good thoughts, pure thoughts, energizing thoughts, thoughts of happy times, funny things that make us laugh, and images of success if life is going to be worth living. But, most of all we should fill our minds with thoughts that allow us to see God moving in His power, as we are being made into someone great and full of success.

We should keep these things in mind and wear them around our necks as a reminder that we are only as powerful as our minds are and that the harvest of our lives is usually a result of the seeds planted in the soil of our thoughts.

SCRIPTURE FOR MEDITATION

Finally, brothers, whatever is true, whatever is noble, whatever is right, whatever is pure, whatever is lovely, whatever is admirable – if anything is excellent or praiseworthy – think about such things.

Philippians 4:8

PRAYER

Dear heavenly Father, I come to you with praise and thanksgiving. I thank you for all the wonderful gifts you have given me. I give you thanks for my mind. You have given me the ability to think. I realize that I should not waste my mind, but use it to its fullest potential. Show me how to think clearly. Teach me how to keep vanity out of my mind. Show me how to fill my mind with pure things and pure thoughts. Amen. .

Personal Journal Thoughts:

How do you view the power of your mind and what can you do in order to produce positive and powerful thoughts?

# Living in Expectations

Don't lower your expectations to meet your performance. Raise your level of performance to meet your expectations.

RALPH MARSTON

Expectations are like roadmaps. What we expect leads us to where we intend to arrive. Even if we get off track at times, our expectations lead us back to the right road of our purpose and aim.

Many people are not failing to reach high and rewarding peaks in life, because they are created to be on the bottom. Some people are where they are in life, simply because they have no real expectation of something greater. Having high expectations is a matter of choice. And, to receive what we expect life to yield is a matter of determination and effort to make something happen.

If we have no expectations we will travel only the roads and ways that life presents, instead of plowing our own way when no way is made for us.

God has given us what we need to plow our own roads when none are available or when our way is blocked, but this can only be accomplished with the power of high expectations.

Without high expectancies of life, we remain where we are or on the road we are traveling that sometimes go nowhere.

SCRIPTURE FOR MEDITATION

Now to him who is able to do immeasurably more than all we ask or imagine, according to his power that is at work within us, to him be glory ...

Ephesians 3:20-21

PRAYER

Lord, thank you for life and for all it offers. You are my God and I put my hope in you. Each morning you give me another chance. You have promised me in your word great things to come. I stand with faith and in expectation to see the manifestations of your promises in my life. Thank you God for those promises that are coming my way! Amen.

Personal Journal Thoughts:

What do you expect out of life? What do you expect from God? What steps will you take in order to reach your expectations?

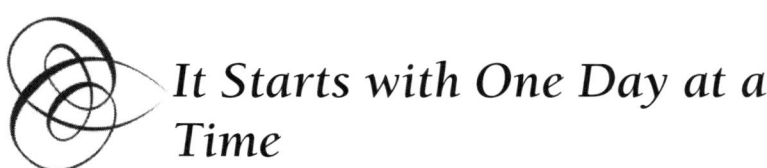# It Starts with One Day at a Time

Men spend their lives in anticipations, in determining to be vastly happy at some period or other, when they have time. But the present time has one advantage over every other: it is our own.

J. N. GEHMAN

Today has started with peace and sunshine. The air is cool and gentle. I'm excited about what this day holds. I realize that about 90% of this day hinges on what I expect, what I look for and what I believe to be true about God, as well as about myself.

I realize that life can take various turns, some good and some bad, but my attitude towards these experiences determines whether my good becomes bad or my bad become good. I believe that God gives us this choice as He gives us the day.

God gives us the choice to have something to do with the making of our days. What an opportunity! What else is faith besides taking hold of the events in our lives through Christ and sharing as partners with God at making the day worthwhile?

But, even participating with God during the day is a matter of choice. If God is willing, tomorrow presents another choice and chance to do something with a day or different. But, we should not spend all of this day worrying about tomorrow, for it will come if it is in the will of the Creator. Instead we should take this day as the greatest opportunity we have. After all is said and done it starts with one day at a time and nothing more. Today is all we have and we must take advantage of it.

SCRIPTURE FOR MEDITATION

So do not worry, saying, "What shall we eat?" or "what shall we drink?" or "What shall we wear?"… your heavenly Father knows that you need them. But seek first his kingdom and his righteousness, and all these things will be given to as well. Therefore, do not worry about tomorrow … each day has enough trouble of its own.

Matthew 6:31-34

PRAYER

Dear heavenly Father, thank you for each day you allow me to experience. I realize that each day is a gift from you. Father, there are times when I grow impatient and attempt to do things on my own without you. Forgive me. Show me how to be still in your presence and listen to your voice. Show me how not to move too fast or move too slow. I know that when I wait for you, you will lead me to greater places in my life according to your divine will. Amen.

Personal Journal Thoughts:

How do you view each day of your life and what do you plan to do with it?

Taking Control of the Direction You Go

Every man gotta right to decide his own destiny.

BOB MARLEY

There are some things in life we cannot control. But the direction our life goes is not one of them. We have whatever we need to aim our lives in a certain direction. The direction in which our lives go is a matter of choice and not by happenstance neither is it determined by the various negative events we face.

The direction we go in life is up to each individual. If we do not take control of our direction, life goes according to the flow of our circumstances and situations. A life without deliberate direction is like sand caught in a high wind which moves in the direction the wind takes it. We should not live like the sand on a beach that is moved by the winds.

We can't control what life brings or issues out, but we can control the direction we allow them to take us. We control the direction our lives goes when we try hard enough to go in the way of our God given potential and essence – life changes according to our direction and our directions change our lives.

SCRIPTURE FOR MEDITATION

But remember the Lord your God, for it is he who gives you the ability to produce wealth, and so confirms his covenant, which he swore to your forefathers, as it is today.

Deuteronomy 8:18

PRAYER

Lord, how great is your name! Thank you Lord for giving me the power to choose! I realize that my life will only go in the direction of the choices I make whether they are negative or positive. Give me wisdom to live life on purpose and not by accident. Guide my feet in the direction of holiness in order that I may live a life pleasing to you. Amen.

Personal Journal Thoughts:

Where are you going? What can you do in order to assure that you control the direction your life goes?

 *Facing God*

While I know myself as a creation of God, I am also obligated to realize and remember that everyone else and everything else are also God's creation.

MAYA ANGELOU

Each morning presents us with the chance to interface with God afresh in some form or another or in some way or another. We are afforded the chance to come into His divine presence, just the way we are – raw! We should rejoice and be glad for such a moment, for to be in the shadows of the Almighty is an awesome privilege that we do not deserve.

The opportunity to interface with God is to come before Him without hiding behind our mask. We can simply come to Him out in the open and trusting that He will take us just the way we are – uncut and uncovered. This can be a scary thing, considering our flaw and failures.

The opportunity to come into God's presence comes with a challenge. And that challenge is to face and try Him at His word

– to trust Him – to get to know Him and to see what great and new things He will do with us and for us.

Facing God is not an easy thing. It's a chance and a challenge – a chance to be blessed beyond our flaws and fears, and the challenge to trust Him when we can't see exactly what He is doing with us. This takes faith. But, what a place to be – in the face of God!

SCRIPTURE FOR MEDITATION

Shout for joy to the Lord, all the earth. Worship the Lord with gladness; come before him with joyful songs. Know that the Lord is God. It is he who made us ... Enter his gates with thanksgiving and his courts with praise ... For the Lord is good and his love endures forever ...

Psalm 100:1-5

PRAYER

Dear heavenly Father, I come to you with thanksgiving and honor. You are the Mighty God the Creator of all things. Your name is worthy of my praise. You cover me under the shadows of your wings. I cannot hide from your presence. Thank you Lord for allowing me to come into your presence just the way I am. By your grace I come before you as an empty cup needing to be filled. Pour into me and renew my heart and my spirit in order that I may glorify your great name. Amen.

Personal Journal Thoughts:

How do you view the presence of God? How do you view yourself when in God's presence? What do you expect from God as you commune with Him?

Life's Notebook

Our life is a book that writes itself and whose principal themes sometimes escape us. We are like characters in a novel who do not always understand what the author wants of them.

JULIEN GREEN

I believe that life should never be like a finished book or a completed novel, for God is not finished writing our lives. There is more to come!

Life should be like a loose leaf notebook, filled with life notes – blessings, moments of favor, times we failed, the mistakes we've made, happy times and sad moments.

It should also be full of blank pages ready to be written on – waiting for new stories, new victories, new successes and even new failures and new and greater expectations.

Life's notebook should be filled with unfinished drafts – after all this is what best sellers are made of – rough draft after rough draft.

God desires to write a new story for each of us, for He is the Author and the Finisher of our lives and faith. So, the best thing to do is to be still and open up and trust Him at His penmanship.

SCRIPTURE FOR MEDITATION

For we are God's workmanship, created in Christ Jesus to do good works, which God prepared in advance for us to do.

Ephesians 2:10

PRAYER

Lord, thank you for my life. I realize that there are many things I have yet to see and experience. There are many places in the world that I have yet to go. There are many people I've yet to meet. Lord, I come to you as a blank page, ready to be written on. I submit to your divine penmanship. You are the Author of my life. As you make the day new, make me new for your glory. Make my life a best seller. Amen.

Personal Journal Thoughts:

As God writes a new script of your life, what will your life look like?

Letter from the Author

Dear Reader,

I hope that you are encouraged by the words printed on these simple pages. The journal entries you have read have been pinned from the deep inkwells of my life. Some of these places were painful and perhaps still are. Some of them were funny, while others have no description.

These words were pinned during the dawning of the day when I sat wondering how I was going to make it through some of the darkest days I've ever faced. Some were written as I sat on planes traveling to different cities and countries. Some of the places I traveled were in my mind, because of a deep longing to escape into some utopia.

These words were composed at a time when I wanted to quit, but God would not allow me to. I couldn't let go of God's promises for my life and for the lives of others.

I have learned through this course of life whether negative or positive, whether at the hands of others or at my own, that if life is going to be fulfilling and exciting – yielding those experiences that may be deemed deeper and meaningful and full of purpose, I had to learn to pray over and over again for something bigger than me and pray for power to attempt something that do not equal my human size or even my resources.

I've learned through painful disappointments, through tricks and trials imposed upon me by others or through my own faults and mistakes, to ask God for something that is bigger than my human abilities and I had to believe that what I asked of Him would be granted to me as I stand firmly in my faith without slipping from the lessons I've learned in my journey. God taught me to believe in receiving the extraordinary.

Through this portion of my journey, I've learned that we should look for what we believe to be true through the eyes of our hearts, even if it takes a while to see it with our human eyes. We must learn to live by faith and not simply by sight.

We must develop the courage to face and fight for something bigger than us and expect to win the fight. It takes faith, courage, effort and determination and the will to live. This is not easy.

Journaling for me was an outlet that kept me from going over the edge. And I hope and pray that something in these pages will encourage you to hold on and not give in or give out, but that you would wait in faith until your change come. And it will come. It may be closer than you realize.

~ **Donald R. Hudson**

About The Author

Dr. Donald R. Hudson

Dr. Donald Hudson is a native of Texas. He has been in the preaching ministry for more than thirty-five years.

He has successfully served as a Senior Pastor in Virginia, Nebraska and Michigan. He currently serves as the Senior Pastor and Founder of the UMOJA Christian Church in Indianapolis, Indiana.

Dr. Hudson has received degrees from several leading colleges and seminaries in the U.S. He has earned the Bachelor of Arts Degree in Biblical Studies and Christian Counseling from the Criswell College for Biblical Studies in Dallas, Texas. He has earned the Master of Divinity Degree and the Doctorate of Ministry Degree from the Samuel Dewitt Proctor School of Theology at the Virginia Union University in Richmond, Virginia.

He has served as an adjunct professor in the studies of Advance Preaching and Theology. He has also served as a lecturer and trainer for World Missions in the area of missions. Due to his passion for justice and equality, he has served in doing missions in several countries outside of the U.S.

He currently shares on various boards and committees for social justice and community revitalization, which has afforded him several awards from various organizations.

He is the author of the book entitled, "Sermonic Connection: Simple Steps Linking the Sermon from the Pulpit to the Pew". He shares as a presenter in major Preaching Conferences, as well as train preaching staffs in the area of homiletics.

Dr. Hudson is married to Leatrice Helena (Cash) Hudson.

In summary, Dr. Hudson contends that "People are vessels of potential and great possibilities and are capable of reaching new levels of life experiences, if they put their mind and heart to it."